Write a Book in Four Weeks

Richter Publishing

Write & Publish a Book Series

(Volume III)

By Tara Richter

LCCN Permalink: https://lccn.loc.gov/2017900083
Library of Congress: 2017900083 - ISBN -13: 978-0692298947

DISCLAIMER

This book is designed to provide information on writing and blogging only. This information is provided and sold with the knowledge that the publisher and author do not offer any legal or medical advice. In the case of a need for any such expertise, consult with the appropriate professional. This book does not contain all information available on the subject. This book has not been created to be specific to any individual's or organization's situation or needs. Every effort has been made to make this book as accurate as possible. However, there may be typographical and/ or content errors. Therefore, this book should serve only as a general guide and not as the ultimate source of subject information. This book contains information that might be dated and is intended only to educate and entertain. The author and publisher shall have no liability or responsibility to any person or entity regarding any loss or damage incurred, or alleged to have incurred, directly or indirectly, by the information contained in this book. You hereby agree to be bound by this disclaimer or you may return this book within the guarantee time period for a full refund. In the interest of full disclosure, this book contains affiliate links that might pay the author or publisher a commission upon any purchase from the company. While the author and publisher take no responsibility for the business practices of these companies and or the performance of any product or service, the author or publisher has used the product or service and makes a recommendation in good faith based on that experience. Any and all references to WordPress including screenshots, is owned solely by them. This is just a reference guide to teach others how to utilize their system. All characters appearing in this work are fictitious. Any resemblance to real persons, living or dead, is purely coincidental.

TESTIMONIES

"I was so excited to be one of Tara's clients to be coached through the writing and publishing process! I have never written a book, so I knew when I wanted to embark on this journey, she was the one I needed to contact. Since she already had three books under her belt, I called her to find out how she did it. I was amazed after our phone conversation that she had discovered a quick and easy way to get a book published in only a few months. I didn't even think that was possible! I knew Kevin and I had to work with her on our project. I really wanted our book to come from the heart and soul so it would resonate with the reader. It was a challenging journey, but Tara's tips and coaching has really made the process a breeze. She's helped us every step of the way and looked out for me; Tara keeps me on track with my goal. If I can write and publish a book with no experience, you can too!" - Anthony Amos Multi Founding franchisor & partnership expert

(http://theanthonyamos.com/)

"When Anthony and I decided to publish a joint book, he said he wanted it to be available for sale within a few months. I thought he was crazy, we wouldn't have enough time in our hectic schedules to get this done. However, when we brought Tara aboard, her coaching techniques made it easy. She has streamlined the writing and publishing process, utilizing every spare minute for maximum results. Even with my super busy schedule I can get a book done. She utilizes every spare second you have. If you want to be a published author, Tara is the one to get the job done!" - Kevin Harrington, Shark from ABC's "Shark Tank"

(http://kevinharrington.tv/

CONTENTS

INTRODUCTION

Whenever I tell people I can help them write a book in four weeks, I always get a look of confusion and dismay. "That can't be done! Books take years and years of methodical research and time consuming edits!" Well the fact is, YES it can be done. We now live in an age of instant gratification and the old ways of writing a book on a typewriter have long passed.

I have helped many authors write and publish their stories in just a few short weeks. The process is truly amazing. The first part is getting over that mental hurdle in your mind that you must work on a novel for ten some years. I think that's a big step for people to overcome. Once you have opened your mind to the process and changed your attitude towards writing and publishing, you will embrace the wonderful new age of quick results.

The methods that I am sharing with you in this guide book are the same principals I give workshops on and teach my authors. Once you take the great feat of writing a book and break it down into small simple steps, anything is possible. When people set forth to climb Mount Kilimanjaro, they do not do it in one big leap, but by putting one foot in front of the other. Most people think writing a book is a huge mountain to overcome, yet they are looking at the top from the bottom. They don't see the small, little steps in front of them that they must begin with.

I have broken down the complex writing process into an easy to follow streamlined process for anyone to write a book in four weeks. It just takes discipline to stay on track. You can't hike half-way up the mountain and then decide it's too much work. Just consistently take the small steps each day and soon you will be on your way to becoming a published author!

Sincerely,

Tara Richter

CHAPTER 1 KEEPING YOUR VOICE

It's a daunting task to sit down and write a book. Most people want to write a book at some point in their lives, whether about their life experiences or for business purposes. I believe as humans we all have the desire to create. The only difference between the authors who publish a book and those who don't is simply taking the time to do it.

There is never a right time to compose a novel. Extra minutes will never just loom over you. You have to create in the chaos. You have to make the time and effort to make it happen. I have written, published, designed, and marketed 100 some books since 2011. I didn't have time to do that while also managing six properties and running a coaching business, but I did. I will share with you my process and how I utilized every minute to make it count.

Some people may think a ghost writer is a better option—that you can just tell your story and have someone else write it. A ghost writer can be a big help, however you want to make sure you find someone that can keep your voice. These are your stories. This is your pain or happiness. No one can fully understand what you have gone through in life, so they cannot accurately express it on paper unless they have the ability to crawl into your brain and feel it from your point of view. Only *you* can. So be careful if you decide to go down the ghost writing path. Make sure you read other books they have published. See if the story resonates with you. Does it move your soul?

I had a ghost writer offer to write my first book, "10 Rules to Survive the Dating Jungle." However, she wanted to make it fiction, and I didn't want to take that direction. The book was a set of rules I made for myself after enduring a divorce, losing my stepson, and surviving an entire lifetime of toxic, unhealthy relationships. She had no idea the pain and agony I went through with a controlling and verbally abusive husband. Or the strength it took to put an end to the manipulation and start loving myself. Only I knew what it felt like. So in order to tell my story, to connect and resonate with the reader, my words had to come from me.

I often get lengthy emails from people who read my books that tell me how much they enjoy hearing my stories. It is great knowing that someone else has gone through the same turmoil and come out on the other end as a positive and healthy person. I have had fans I've never met wave me down at conventions and share their own stories with me. Why? Because they felt a connection with me when reading my words.

Instead of reading a book, it was as if they were sitting down with their girlfriend exchanging stories over a cup of coffee. That is what gets you loyal followers. Once you make that deep personal connection with someone, they will never forget who you are. You will hold a special place in their hearts because they understand what you have been through, how you succeeded, and what mark you've made on earth.

I knew a lady who went through a very tragic experience as a child, with a great story to tell. I was intrigued while talking to her, and I really wanted to read her book. When I acquired a copy, I couldn't wait to get home to read it. I was truly disappointed. After muddling through only a chapter I had to put it down. It was so bad. You could tell the ghost writer was a decent writer, but the pain could not make a connection with me. A story of tremendous catastrophe should have been flooded with deep emotions. It should have made me cry. I wanted the book to take me down that emotional rollercoaster, but the ghost writer couldn't pull it off. I tried reading it five times and, well, to be honest I still haven't finished it. It's a shame, too. It would have been a great book if it would have come from her own heart and soul.

Within my publishing house, we have taken many ghost written stories that were mutilated and pulled them back together and polished them off. It is not an easy task to do and then the author ends up paying more to actually get the book done. So do your research first before hiring someone to help you out.

You might be afraid to put your story out there, and I do admit it's a grueling process. There is no short cut to get it done, but I will provide tips and tricks that will make it easier. Once you start writing you will probably hate what you put down on paper. It's going to look ugly and stink. It's okay. Don't worry about your book being perfect—that's what editing is for. The most important thing is to get it out of your head and on paper! Just get it out. Don't censor yourself and don't edit—not even the spelling or grammar. I know once you get your creative juices flowing, your fingers will not type fast enough to get all the thoughts out of your head! That's the best feeling: once you find that sweet spot within you. It may take a little bit to discover what works best for you.

For example, I like to sit with my laptop looking out a window at the beautiful ocean (luckily enough I live in Florida!) alone, with the TV off, playing music in the background. That is my creative sweet spot. However, I do write in odd and peculiar places as well, such as standing in line at the grocery store, on airplanes, and while walking on the treadmill. I know, sounds crazy right? It is crazy... but it works.

Take advantage of every spare moment you have to finish your book. Write when you feel inspired. Once your thoughts are spinning in your head you need to stop what you're doing and write them down, even if the notes are chicken scratch. If you don't, you may forget them, or the thoughts will not be as intense as they were at the moment you first felt them.

I composed my second and third books in small chunks writing everywhere you could imagine. I used the notepad app on my iPhone. I even bought a fifty dollar Bluetooth keyboard so I can easily sit and write when I'm inspired. Once I'm done with my thoughts I email it to myself so when I get home, it's waiting in my inbox. Then I copy and paste it into a Word document and clean It up.

Anytime you have an extra five minutes in your day, you need to write. Waiting in line to pick up the kids from school? Write on your smartphone or tablet. Walking on the treadmill? Jot some ideas down. I get some of my best ideas while working out, probably because of all the blood pumping through my veins and those feel-good endorphins flooding my body.

Traveling soon? Airports are another great place to write. Just think about how many minutes you waste lining up to be groped by security, waiting for delayed flights, or sitting on the plane while the staff fuels up, thinking, *Damn, where is that truck to push back the plane?*

One summer I was on a flight heading from Tampa to Nebraska with my cool little portable Bluetooth keyboard with me. I was typing away on my iPhone, listening to music, and having a grand 'ole time. An elderly couple next to me was staring out of the corner of their eyes, trying, but failing, to be sly. Finally, I took my earbuds out so they could ask me their obvious question, "What is this setup you have going on?" I told them that I'm an author, that I compose most of my books with this mini keyboard linked to my smartphone. They were amazed.

I have tried using the voice dictation option on my iPhone and my experience is that it does not work well. It doesn't understand what I'm saying and it makes more errors than it's worth. Also, I realized that when I'm writing and thinking of what I want to say and how to say it, I pause and re-organize the thoughts in my head a lot. When I do this verbally it also makes for a messy transcription to clean up. When I'm typing, I have more time to adjust my information while it goes from my brain, to my fingertips, to my laptop. Typing works better for me than speaking does. There may be better voice-to-text software out there, and that may be an easier option for you. I'm sure the technology will get better in the future. It doesn't really matter how you do it, just find your sweet spot. That's the key.

DON'T EDIT WHILE YOU WRITE

While you are composing your book, don't worry about formatting, editing, or how it looks in Word. Sometimes you will get caught up in those details, but it's more important to get the thoughts out of your head and on paper. Cleaning it up, editing, and formatting will be done during revisions. Your first document is a rough draft. They call it that for a reason. It's rough. It's probably going to suck at some points, but that's okay. No one writes a perfect book the first time around. Just get the concept and ideas out of your head, no matter how awful you think it might be at the time. Once you get into the writing flow, sometimes phrases come out of your mind faster than your fingers can type. So things can get chopped up and not make sense, but that's what an editor is for—another person's perspective. Your job is just to write!

USE GOOGLE FOR SPELLING

Just as I'm writing this an issue came up, one that has happened almost daily. Word does not have the best spelling and grammar system, especially when it comes to new technology terms. Their program is not updated enough. Or maybe it's a lack of me installing the updates. Whatever it is, Word does not recognize many new words. Just as I was typing "earbuds," Word underlines it in red and tells me it's misspelled. So I end up Googling the word to see how it is spelled. As I assumed, I was right, Word was wrong. Funny enough, it underlines "Googling" as misspelled too. So don't always trust Word. Google is a much more up-to-date source. I'm constantly going back and forth between Google and Word while I'm writing. I do it unconsciously. It occurred to me that not everyone would know that trick, especially if you are not an avid writer.

Review:

Tip 1: Create in chaos.

Tip 2: Utilize every minute by using smartphones, tablets, or notepads.

Tip 3: Stop what you're doing and write down your thoughts as soon as you are inspired.

Tip 4: Use Google for spelling.

2

CHAPTER 2 GETTING ORGANIZED

The most important thing to do before you start writing is to organize your thoughts. How do you write a book in four weeks? By using a detailed outline. Yes, there is a method to the madness. An outline will help you do two things:

1. Help the flow of your book.

2. Take an easy first step into a difficult and daunting writing process.

An industry standard 5 x 8, 100 page book is approximately 20,000 words. That's 20,000 words you would need to write in a four week period. Without structure, those words will loom over you. 20,000?! How can I write 20,000 words in four weeks?!

Easy manageable steps, that's how. Use an accountability calendar. Turn that gluttonous meal into smaller chewable chunks. 20,000 words? That's 715 words per day. You can have a finished rough draft in only 28 days. Phew! Doesn't that sound like a breeze? **715 x 28 = 20,020**

WRITE A BOOK IN 4 WEEKS!

1 Goal: 715	2 Goal: 715	3 Goal: 715	4 Goal: 715	5 Goal: 715	6 Goal: 715	7 Tally: 5,005
Actual:	Actual:	Actual:	Actual:	Actual:	Actual:	Actual Tally:
8 Goal: 715	9 Goal: 715	10 Goal: 715	11 Goal: 715	12 Goal: 715	13 Goal: 715	14 Tally: 10,010
Actual:	Actual:	Actual:	Actual:	Actual:	Actual:	Actual Tally:
15 Goal: 715	16 Goal: 715	17 Goal: 715	18 Goal: 715	19 Goal: 715	20 Goal: 715	21 Goal: 15,015
Actual:	Actual:	Actual:	Actual:	Actual:	Actual:	Actual Tally:
22 Goal: 715	23 Goal: 715	24 Goal: 715	25 Goal: 715	26 Goal: 715	27 Goal: 715	28 Goal: 20,020
Actual:	Actual:	Actual:	Actual:	Actual:	Actual:	Actual Tally:

BOOK OUTLINE

Utilize a detailed outline. Breaking down the subject matter of the books into multiple chapters and sub-chapters will help you when coming up with your content. It also lets you know what information comes at what point in the book, so it flows in the traditional book format. Remember this is only for CliffsNotes.

Title Page – Includes title, authors, and editors.

Dedication – Who do you want to dedicate your book to?

_____

_____

_____

_____

_____

_____

Table of Contents – This part will be created during the formatting process in another course.

Foreword – Usually written by someone with more experience in your industry than yourself. _____

_____

_____

Acknowledgements – Who would you like to give credit to for helping the book become a reality? Ex. Mentors, Graphic Designers, Ghost Writers, etc. _____

_____

_____

_____

Introduction – Short synopsis of what the entire book is about. It only needs to be a few pages long. _____

_____

_____

_____

_____

_____

Chapter 1 – Subject:_____

_____

_____

_____

Chapter 1 – Subchapter _____

_____

_____

Chapter 1 – Subchapter_____

_____

_____

Chapter 1 – Subchapter_____

_____

_____

Chapter 2 – Subject:_____

_____

_____

Chapter 2 – Subchapter _____

_____

_____

Chapter 2 – Subchapter_____

_____

_____

Chapter 2 – Subchapter_____

_____

_____

Chapter 3 – Subject:_____

_____

_____

Chapter 3 – Subchapter _____

_____

_____

Chapter 3 – Subchapter_____

_____

_____

Chapter 3 – Subchapter_____

_____

_____

Chapter 4 – Subject:_____

_____

_____

Chapter 4 – Subchapter _____

_____

_____

Chapter 4 – Subchapter_____

_____

_____

Chapter 4 – Subchapter_____

_____

_____

Chapter 5 – Subject:_____

_____

_____

Chapter 5 – Subchapter _____

_____

_____

Chapter 5 – Subchapter_____

_____

_____

Chapter 5 – Subchapter_____

_____

_____

Chapter 6 – Subject:_____

_____

_____

Chapter 6 – Subchapter _____

_____

_____

Chapter 6 – Subchapter_____

_____

_____

Chapter 6 – Subchapter_____

_____

_____

Chapter 7 – Subject:_____

_____

_____

Chapter 7 – Subchapter _____

_____

_____

Chapter 7 – Subchapter_____

_____

_____

Chapter 7 – Subchapter_____

_____

_____

Chapter 8 – Subject:_____

_____

_____

Chapter 8 – Subchapter _____

_____

_____

Chapter 8 – Subchapter_____

_____

_____

Chapter 8 – Subchapter_____

_____

_____

Chapter 9 – Subject:_____

_____

_____

Chapter 9 – Subchapter _____

_____

_____

Chapter 9 – Subchapter_____

_____

_____

Chapter 9 – Subchapter_____

_____

_____

Chapter 10 – Subject:_____

_____

Chapter 10 – Subchapter _____

_____

_____

Chapter 10 – Subchapter_____

_____

_____

Chapter 10 – Subchapter_____

_____

_____

Final Thoughts/ Summary – A few pages to tie it all up._____

_____

_____

_____

_____

_____

Author Bio & Photo – Use professional pictures. Keep it short and put

links to businesses, other books, etc. _____

_____

_____

_____

_____

_____

_____

_____

_____

_____

_____

_____

_____

_____

_____

_____

_____

_____

_____

_____

_____

Review:

Tip 1: Use an accountability calendar and detailed outline. Download the forms from our website here:

http://richterpublishing.com/resources/

Tip 2: Write 715 words per day.

Tip 3: Fill out the outline prior to writing. Every day, sit down and write, tackling one section of the outline a day.

3

CHAPTER 3 SECTIONS OF A BOOK

Let's talk small. I know I just tossed you an outline, and you're thinking, "Whoa! Disclaimer? Dedication? Copyright? Slow down, slow down. I'm still stuck on the title!"

Don't fret. Those sections and subsections in the outline are there to help organize your thoughts. In this chapter, you will learn what is needed in each one. You will know how to pick a winning title, what to focus on chapter by chapter, who to include in your acknowledgements, etc. It is important to not only know all the sections of a book, but what always goes into those sections. People get confused and mix up things like the introduction and preface. They are not the same. Use the information in this chapter to get the right pieces into the correct parts of the puzzle.

Utilize this information in conjunction with your outline. By the end of this chapter, you will know the format of your book from back to front. I want you to feel the book coming together easy as pie!

THE TITLE PAGE

The title page is the very first page within a printed book. It also lists the author, possibly even the editors. Title is one of the most important aspects of your book. Your title will be a major selling point. You don't need to have your title now however. Sometimes, the title comes after you have written most of the book—and that's just fine. The title is something that needs to catch the eye of a potential reader. It's like the billboard for your book. How can you grab someone's attention in 5 seconds or less? Pull them in, make them stop and think. When I go to big conventions to sell my author's books and look for new aspiring writers, I have a big banner that says, "Write a Book in 4 Weeks." The title of this book. It's literally a banner with those few words and a big pile of colorful books. It makes people stop and think, then they laugh out loud a little, but then they walk over and ask me how? That's what you want your book to do. What few words can make people stop dead in their tracks and become curious?

Here are a few great existing titles to inspire you:

- Failing Successfully: Life After Debt (*financial book*)
- The Asshole Survival Guide
- Old as Dirt & Sexy as Hell (*health & fitness book*)
- OMG WTF!? What's the Focus? (*business book*)
- Pink Hell: Breast Cancer Sucks

Now some of these make you laugh, and some make you think and say to yourself, "Ya I know a few assholes." Make it make you stop and focus on that book. Think of the books you have read, the titles that you like. Sometimes having a little controversy with them isn't a bad thing either. There are a million books on Amazon, what is going to make yours stand out?

Also do your research and start searching titles in Amazon, Google, etc. If there are many books with a similar title, then you need to change it up. Because once it's published and people go in and search your title, you don't want all these other similar books pulling up in the search engine. Make it easy for people to find you. If people have to click more than two or three times they usually just give up. Sad but true.

For example my author from Denmark's title translated into English exactly as, "You Are Worthier." At first it sounded odd, however when I started researching, NO ONE had that EXACT same title. How cool is that? So it's very easy to locate. Now if you search "You Are Worthy" a whole crap load of books pull up. So you can also do a play on words or move things around. With the title you have to be thinking from a marketing standpoint. It may not always be proper grammar but that doesn't matter for a title. It's about branding. Example: iPhone, iPad, Apple made those words up. Guess what? You can too!

Remember: Bounce around ideas with friends, family members, and business associates. If you keep your title idea to yourself, you may not recognize when it might need changing.

If you have not already, find a writer's meet-up group in your area. It's a great resource to be around like-minded people. Who knows?

Maybe there's an author in your area who will suddenly blurt out the perfect title for your book.

To share ideas, join our private Facebook writing and publishing group: https://www.facebook.com/groups/651297888241700/

COPYRIGHT

Many authors have questions about the copyright process to protect your manuscript. Now, I am not an attorney. I am not giving legal advice. You would need to speak to an attorney for any specific details. From what I know, once your book is published with a set publication date, you are secured on the copyright of its content.

However, if you want to completely secure the book content, you can visit http://www.copyright.gov/ and pay to have the book recorded within the United States Copyright office. It's $55 per title. In my company we file the copyright for all of our books after they publish. So then we can mail in a copy that will be stored within the Library of Congress.

This is an example of a general copyright that we use within all of our books:

Copyright © 2014 Tara Richter

All rights reserved. No part of this book may be reproduced in any form by any electronic or mechanical means (including photocopying, recording or information storage and retrieval) without permission in writing from the author. For permissions email xyz@gmail.com.

The copyright laws are different in other countries. From http://www.copyright.gov/fls/fl100.html:

"There is no such thing as an 'international copyright' that will automatically protect an author's writings throughout the world. Protection against unauthorized use in a particular country depends on the national laws of that country."

DISCLAIMER

I recommend everyone put a disclaimer on their book. It is a document—rather, a statement—that waives you of any responsibility for anything that may happen due to someone reading your book.

For example, for my Dating Jungle Series, the disclaimer said that I was not a licensed psychologist or therapist, that I was not giving any medical advice, that I was instead offering my own stories about what worked for me in the dating world.

I have a disclaimer on my website you can download and customize specifically for your book: http://richterpublishing.com/resources/

You may want to have an attorney review the disclaimer on your behalf.

DEDICATION

You are recognizing the people you want to dedicate your book to. Generally, friends, family, and loved ones. For my Dating Jungle Series, I wrote a humorous dedication to every one of my bad romances, and especially to my ex-husband. However, most people dedicate their book to their spouse, or their mother and father. The dedication should be short, only a few sentences.

ACKNOWLEDGEMENTS

You are recognizing the people that helped your book become a reality. It is easier to pinpoint who you would like to thank in this section. Usually, the people under this category are:

- Editors
- Graphic Designers
- Publishers
- Mentors
- Anyone who gave you information, research, content, etc.
- Anyone who inspired you to write

FOREWORD

A foreword is written by someone other than you. Someone who has more experience in your industry and can give your book credibility. Not every book has a foreword. This is a personal decision for you and your book. However, if you know someone, why not use them? They will raise the profile of your book. For example my authors have been able to contact people such as:

- Barry Alvarez, Director of Athletics University of Wisconsin
- Rocky Bleier, four-time Super Bowl-winning Pittsburgh Steeler running back
- Kevin Harrington, Shark from ABC's Shark Tank
- Jeff Hoffman Co-Founder of Priceline.com

Getting a celebrity endorsement and/or foreword written may not be as hard as it sounds. Many of these people still handle their own social media accounts where you can send a short and sweet message. For example, to get the testimony for this book, I asked Kevin Harrington if he would do an endorsement for the book and he agreed. So I sent him a PDF copy of the book then said, "This is my suggestion of what we could print." I then wrote out the endorsement myself and just got his approval to run with it. You can do the same for the foreword. Write it for them. Then send it to them and ask if they approve. Theis caliber of people are very busy and they do not have time to write something out. Most of the time you can get their secretary or personal assistant to verify everything for you. Then to show your appreciation, send them 10 copies of the book once it is published with a nice thank you card.

INTRODUCTION/ PREFACE

An introduction does not need to be long. It should summarize what your book is about. Think about this section as the "pitch" to your book. Many people will flip to the intro of a book to decide if they want to purchase it. In other words, this section is for you to appeal to potential customers. A good introduction will sell your work to a bigger audience.

Your introduction must capture a few points to the reader:

- What will they gain by reading it?
- How will it change their life?
- How will they become a better, stronger, smarter person?
- What's in it for them?

PROLOGUE

The prologue is different than an introduction of a book. Once again you do not necessarily have to have a prologue in your book. I think they are more for fiction books not so much for non-fiction. However, this is your preference. A prologue usually consists of an act or scene of the storyline to introduce the reader to the type of writing style and point of view.

CHAPTERS

Now we are getting into the "meat" of the book. All the pieces that come before the chapters are called the "front matter." They are all important aspects of the book. However, page one does not start until the first chapter. All the front matter is indexed as roman numerals since it's not really part of the content.

I like to stick with 10 chapters in my books. Think about your topic. Think about how you can divide the information into 10 different sections. The information is easier to understand because it's in smaller sizable chunks. Personally, I like to think about the 10 main points I will cover before I even begin writing.

By dividing your book into sections, the overall writing experience is made easier. All each chapter needs is 10 pages, give or take. The goal is smaller, more attainable. Don't worry if you write too much on one section and write too little in the next. The information can always be changed and divided up later. The original sections are only there to get your creative juices flowing.

Break down the chapters even further into sub-chapters. The more you can slice up the information, the easier it is for readers to digest.

For example, if your book topic is Marketing, you can then break Marketing down to: Online Marketing, Social Media Marketing, TV Marketing, Radio, Billboards, Click Funnels, Pay Per Click Ads, Search Engines, etc. Then break down Social Media Marketing chapter into subtopics; Facebook, Instagram, LinkedIn, and so on.

Remember to incorporate personal stories to help prove your point. You don't want your information to get too dry. As human beings, we connect by understanding each other's struggles. It becomes easier for the reader to identify with you, because your message is now twice as powerful.

My favorite thing to do at the end of a chapter is to write bullet points summarizing what readers should take away from the chapter. You can call it 'Chapter Tips,' 'Chapter Review,' 'Chapter Summary,' really, whatever you like. You are organizing the information, almost like CliffsNotes. Let's face it, we live in an "instant gratification" society. Who has the time to read a 12,000 page "War & Peace" novel? At least your readers can read the highlight of each chapter if they don't have the time to dig deep into the content.

If you must have a large book, I recommend one of two things:

1. Breaking it up into a 2 or 3 book series.
2. Making the Table of Contents as descriptive as possible.

Choose wisely.

SUMMARY/ FINAL THOUGHTS/ EPILOGUE

At the end of your book, it is a good idea to have a "Summary" or "Final Thoughts" section to tie up all of the book's information. If you included a personal journey throughout your story, tell the reader where you are now in life. In the few months you wrote this book, different things could have happened during that time period. End with a "Here I am now..." or a "This is what I learned..."

Maybe you are planning on writing a series. Here, you want to segue into one of the other books. Make it easy for the reader to find your other books.

If you used a prologue in the beginning of your book, then you should use the epilogue to be consistent with style. If you used just an introduction then I would stick to the summary / final thoughts.

AUTHOR'S BIO

The very last section of your book is the author's biography. In the bio you want to include a high resolution photograph. The picture has to have a minimum of 300 DPI (Dots Per Inches). Now, a computer image typically has a DPI of 72 you can use that but the published photo will look fuzzy. A professional photo is 1200 DPI. Go professional.

On this page, include your credentials. What makes you an expert on what you are writing about? Do you have a degree? Have you taught classes? Do you have any radio or TV interviews on your subject? Does your company specialize on this topic? List your website, contact info, related products, etc.

BACK COVER

Potential readers learn from reading your back cover. It is another selling point to gather more readers.

It could be quick, simple snippets of information. Bullet points, for example. In my first "Dating Jungle" book, I used short phrases: "Take control of your dating life!" "Learn the art of flirting!" Anthony Amos' "How to Catch a Shark" utilized a more narrative approach. It reads like a descriptive movie-trailer style blurb.

Once more people read your book, the back cover is a good place to place short reviews. On my third book "5 Steps to Heal a Broken Heart," the back cover features an in-depth review from Dr. Winn Parker, PhD, a member of the American Society of Clinical Pathology. The testimonial gives my book credence. That added credibility is what might push a reader to purchase my book.

Review:

Tip 1: Keep the Introduction short. Write it like a business pitch.

Tip 2: Include a Disclaimer for legal purposes.

Tip 3: Secure a Copyright to protect your intellectual property.

Tip 4: Write chapters in easily digestible chunks.

Tip 5: Take high DPI photographs for the Author's Bio page. No iPhone bathroom selfies.

CHAPTER 4 EDITING

Every book needs an editor. Even if you are a professional writer, you need a different pair of eyes reading your words. When you are the one writing, you are too involved in the process and story. You need another person looking at the content with a fresh mind to see if the story runs smoothly. Does it make sense or did you leave big gaps of information that confuse the reader? And, of course, spelling and grammar also need to be reviewed. One of the writer's biggest mistakes is misusing "their" and "there." When you write certain words, they might look and sound correct, but may not actually be the proper use of the word.

Editors can be very expensive. They charge a variation of prices, anywhere from .09 cents a word and up. When I was writing my first book I didn't have thousands of dollars to spend on a fancy editor with a huge resume and tons of books published. I wasn't sure what to do. I thought about having my mom edit my book, but it was a very personal story about my dissolving marriage and I really didn't want family reading it. Normally I would not recommend a family member editing your book, but mine had a degree in English so she was qualified.

I decided I would hire an intern to do the editing. I thought about going to colleges to find one, but I knew it could have been a lengthy process. I wanted to get someone quickly so I put an ad on Craigslist for a local intern. A few days later I received a response from Casey Cavanagh, who graduated college with a degree in writing. She had a fulltime job but wanted to publish a book herself, so she thought it would be good experience. It was a win-win!

I hired her as an intern to edit my book for less expensive than I would have been able to find elsewhere. Since I was not paying her as much to do this, I credited her on the cover and inside of my book. Plus, I listed her as the editor on Amazon, where my books are sold. I also gave her copies of my books once they were published.

You can even get a few interns. The more eyes you have looking at your work the better. There are many writer meet-up groups, too (www.meetup.com). I've seen some in my local area where it's just for people reviewing other people's work. Usually, it's free. If you are married, have your spouse read it over just for another point of view. I am going to hand over this technical guide to my mom to edit during her winter vacation in Florida. She was a teacher, and is excellent with grammar. In high school and college, she wasn't afraid to rip apart my papers and short stories. She handed them back with red pen marks bleeding all over the page. Utilize all your resources!

SELF-EDITING

Incorporate self-editing. Go through the edits, and either accept or reject them. Be prepared to read your book ten times before it's published. By the time I print my books I'm so sick of reading them I never want to look at them again. But that's the process.

Read your book backwards. Mistakes will pop out at you because your brain is tricked into seeing the words differently. When you read from beginning to end, you know the story. Your brain skims over the paragraphs. *"Yeah, yeah. I've heard this a million times before!"* But if you start at the end, your brain will work harder to understand it.

DON'T EDIT FOREVER

Editing can be very time consuming. Your manuscript may feel like it will never be finished. There will always be things you could add, change, or rephrase. Don't get stuck editing forever. Make a stopping point. Give yourself a deadline. I usually set a book launch party before I have my book done just to force myself to put the pen down and stop.

Three edits from each person is a good goal. You are going to write it and read it, then pass it off to the editor. They then read and edit it. That's one pass through. Then you go over their edits, pass it back to another editor for them to review. That's two passes. Do not do this process more than three times.

The thing is, nothing is ever perfect. Someone will always catch something, or not like the description. I've read books that came from major publishers with errors in them. No one is perfect. Editing forever can be a way of putting off getting your book out there because you're afraid. You think everyone will laugh at you and say your book is crap. I was scared to death to put my first book out there because it talked about all my past relationships. I bared my soul for everyone to judge me. It's not easy, but just do it. Believe me, you will be happy when you do.

I had my first book edited by two people in addition to the edits I did myself. A publisher read it and found ten errors. Not too shabby, considering it was about 150 pages. I really thought there might be more. The point is that nothing is ever going to be perfect, so don't wait to publish until your book is "perfect." Set a deadline and stick to it! Plus with books being print on demand now days, you can always go back and make changes even after it's on distribution channels.

QUESTIONS TO ASK AN EDITOR

Remember, you are the one hiring the editor. This is a job, even if it's an internship position. You are the boss, they are the employee. Make sure you are both on the same page before you get down and dirty with edits. Ask these questions to make sure they are a right fit for you:

1) **Vision** – After discussing your book ,what is their vision of it? Where do they think it should go? Do you both agree on the outcome? Is it fiction or non-fiction?

2) **Experience** – What experience do they have? What books have they edited? If they mostly work on a Vampire Drama series, they might not be the one to edit a technical manual.

3) **Education** – What is their college degree in? They should at least be studying English, Journalism, or Creative Writing. Obviously you don't want a Physical Therapy major who's just looking for a summer job to earn some extra cash.

4) **Software** – You need to make sure you both have the same systems. If you have an IBM utilizing Word, they need the same. If you are using Mac with Pages, they need the same. Otherwise, passing documents back and forth will be a nightmare.

5) **Non-Disclosure Agreement** – Ask them if they are willing to sign a non-disclosure agreement stating they will not distribute or use any ideas, concepts, and so forth from your writings. You need to trust the person with your intellectual property since they will have your original files. Having them sign a non-disclosure agreement will let them know you're serious about keeping your work confidential. If they will not sign one, find a new editor.

6) **Time Frame** – Let them know when you want the book finished. Make sure they have enough available time on their schedule if you need it done quickly.

7) **Age and Gender** – This can be a factor. For my Dating Series, a

sixty-five year old lady is going to have different opinions on dating versus a twenty-one-year-old woman. You don't want to constantly battle over the advice given in your books. Once again this comes back to vision. It's not their book, it's yours! I opted to have a man do the first set of edits because I was a woman giving dating advice, and I wanted to see the man's opinion on them. It worked out well for me. Having an editor that's in your target reader audience is good. Not necessary, but a plus.

PRINT OUT A HARD COPY

At least once during the editing process, print out a copy to review. For some reason you will pick up on mistakes you didn't catch while on the computer. Plus you want to see what it's going to look like printed (the fonts, spacing, photos, etc.). You don't need to do this with every revision, but definitely do it at least once. Keep it in a binder and date it. This is also good evidence for when you are writing the book, just in case some crazy person comes out of the woods claiming you plagiarized their novel. You never know with people being so sue-happy. In my mortgage days I had a "cover-my-ass" folder on my computer, documenting processes for when co-workers or supervisors asked me to do something. If I got in trouble, I would pull up my "CMA" file and read off the dates and times of who said what to the boss. That always got me out of sticky situations!

Review:

Tip #1: Hire interns for editors.

Tip #2: Find free writer meet-ups that review each other's work.

Tip #3: Self-edit by reading backwards.

Tip #4: Do 3 revisions—max.

Tip #5: Set a deadline for your book and stick to it!

CHAPTER 5 TRACK CHANGES

When you are going back and forth with your editor, make sure to use the Track Changes feature in Word. Utilizing this feature, and telling your editor upfront how you want it done, can save you a lot of headaches down the road.

This feature allows one person to make changes, but you have to review and accept them before it's permanent in your document. It will look a little messy, with lots of red lines and edit marks, and it will take some time to go through and review each edit. However, you don't want the editor making permanent changes without your approval. They may understand something wrong that you don't agree with. If you don't track the changes, you may overlook something they changed and it could slip through the cracks. I have heard nightmarish stories where authors gave their manuscript to an editor that chopped it up so bad it turned into an entirely different book. You don't want that.

The job of an editor is to check grammar, spelling, and overall flow of the storyline. Does it make sense? Is every concept described so the reader fully understands? Are facts or information missing, making the plot confusing? It is not their job to re-write the book. Make this clear in the beginning. And of course always keep an original copy on your computer in case you need to go back and start over.

*Also, in order to use the Track Changes feature in Word, you must own a fully licensed version of it. You cannot get away with Word Starter, the free version. Make sure you and your editor both own one.

HOW TO USE TRACK CHANGES

1. Open the document you wish to revise.
2. Click on the Review tab at the top of Microsoft Word.

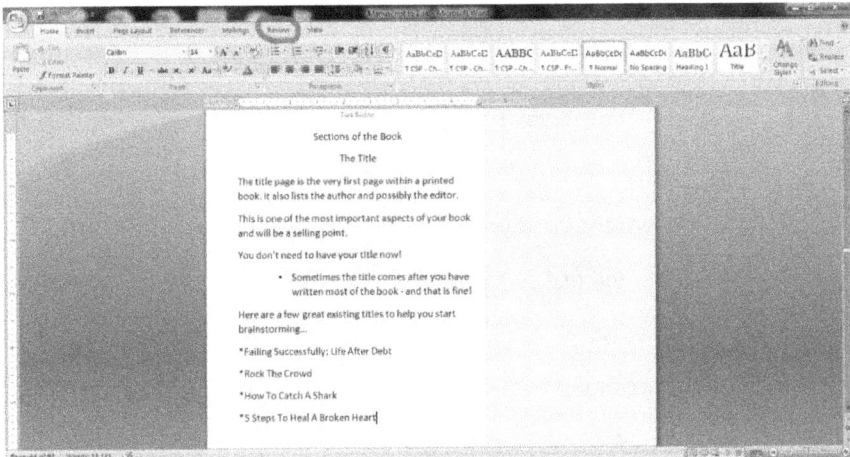

3. Notice the many options under the Review tab. You can use spell check, the thesaurus, word count, etc. The main tools we will focus on are in the sections labeled Comments, Tracking, and Changes.

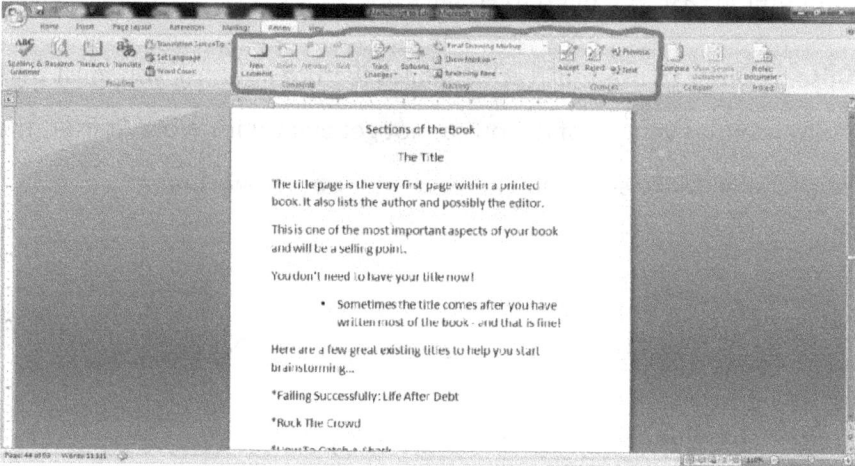

4. Click on the Track Changes button.

   a. If the button stays highlighted, then you are officially using the Track Changes mode. Try it out.

5. Implement your edits on the document. Everything you revise will not permanently affect the document. Once your editor sends you the edits back, you can decide if the changes take effect.

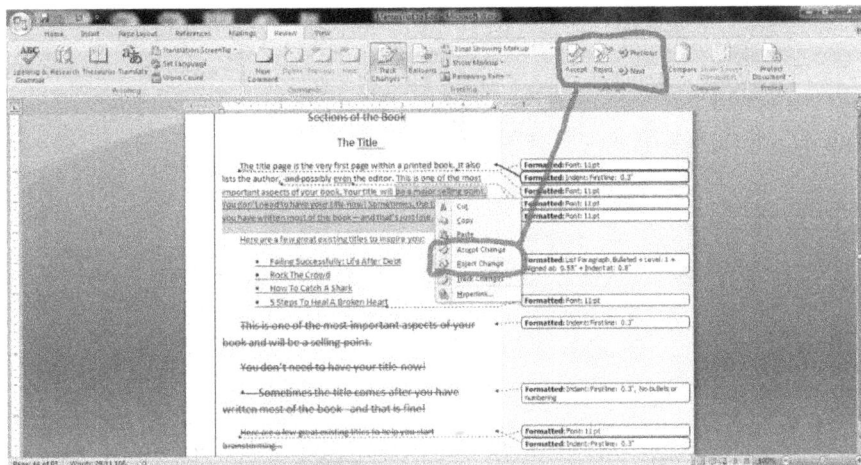

a. Notice the options on the Changes section of the Review tab. There you can Accept or Reject a change. On the right, Previous and Next can be used to find the nearest edit without scavenging through the document.

    i. If you would like to affect *all* of the edits, under those respective buttons there is the nuclear option to Accept or Reject all changes in the document. However, use this option wisely as you can not go back.

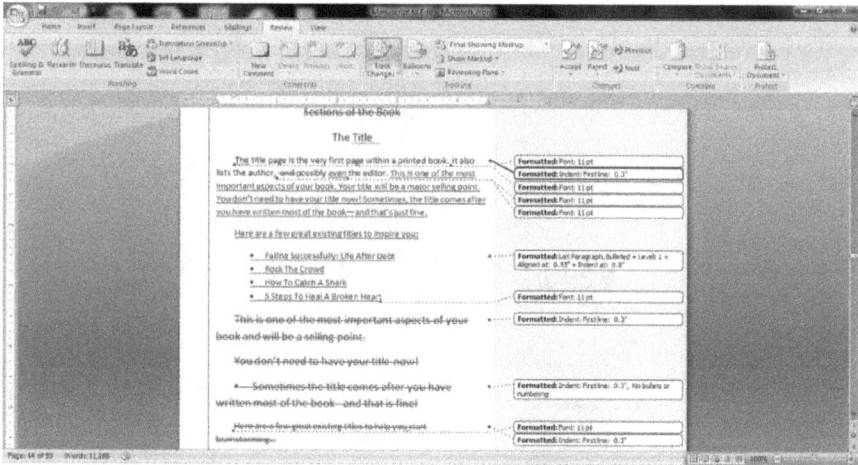

b. Notice the "racking section. Under Balloons you can decide how you want the edits to look.

    i. Balloons: where the edits are labeled on the side of the document.

    ii. Inline: where the edits are unlabeled, instead shown within the document.

    iii. Comments/Formatting: the middle ground. Formatting changes are labeled in balloons, but other edits happen inline.

c. Next to Balloons on the Tracking section, you have a few more options to play with.

    i. Final Showing Markup: decide whether you even see the edits at all.

    ii. Show Markup: Pick and choose what edits you would like to see. You can also choose to view edits performed by one editor and not the others.

iii. Reviewing Pane: Tool to help keep track of what changes were performed on your document.

d. Under Track Changes, you can customize the way edits appear in a document, individualizing the edits to distinguish them from editor to editor.

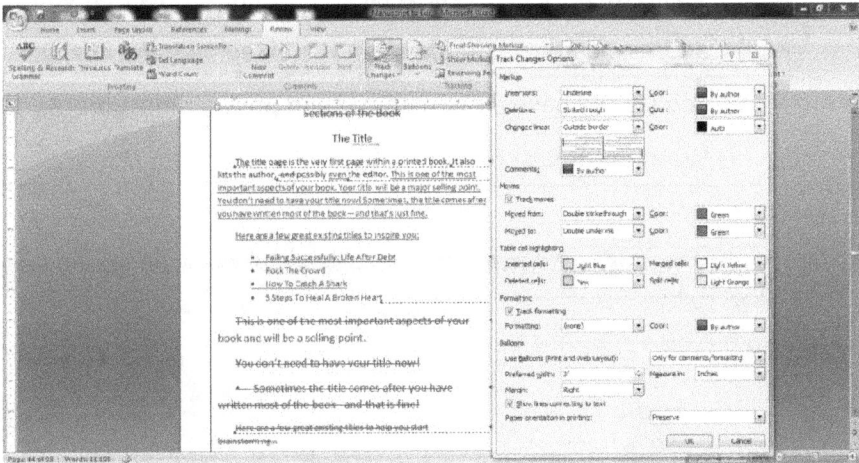

e. Under the Comments section, you can leave comments for whomever is going to read your documents. This is a great feature. Sometimes you cannot call your editor out of the blue to ask them a question about Pg. 45. Comments can help you communicate issues you or the editors might have about your work.

    i. Notice the Previous and Next buttons. If you would like to address every comment, but do not have the patience to scroll through your document until you find one, these buttons are a godsend. They will dart you from comment to comment with total ease.

6. Voila! Now that you know all your options, now that you addressed every comment, and stressed over the changes, you should have a clean edited and polished document. Wasn't that easy?

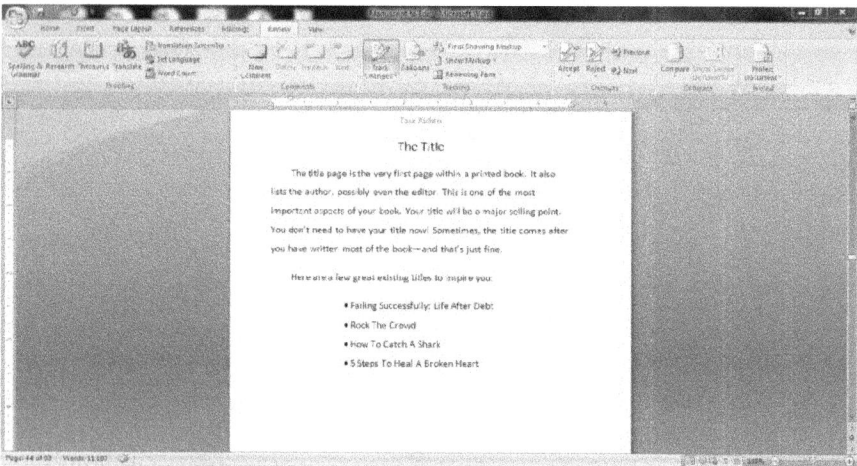

Review:

Tip #1: Use the Track Changes feature under the Review Tab.

Tip #2: Customize how you would like to approach the edits using the features under the Tracking section.

Tip #3: Utilize the Comment options to communicate with your editors.

Tara Richter

CHAPTER 6 BECOME AN EXPERT BY PUBLISHING

Publishing a book is the fastest, easiest way to establish yourself as an expert in your industry. Why? Because if you have 20,000 words to talk about a topic, you must have a lot of experience, whether it is through work experience, life experience, or plain old research.

Choose your book topic carefully. Once you write a book about it, you WILL be considered an expert in that field. Entrepreneurs are usually talented in multiple areas. If you wear multiple hats, make sure you know which area you want to be considered an expert in.

Multiple books published emphasize your expertise. One book makes you an expert. Many books ensures everyone knows you are not going away anytime soon. This is why I published short manuals like this one about writing and publishing. I have 10 books published, which makes me an expert in the writing and publishing field. Plus I can give them out at networking events or conferences because someone may throw away your business card, but they will not toss out a book!

BOOKS RAISE YOUR ONLINE PROFILE

You are who Google says you are. When you publish a book, it will be listed on various distribution channels all over the internet. This enhances your "Googleability."

Googleability is your online presence. For business purposes, you want positive stuff to pop up under your name. In this day and age, the first thing people do is Google someone. The company, the person, their book. A book is a way to positively add to your Googleability.

See my example on the next page. When I "Google" my name, Tara Richter, the first page of Google is everything to do with me: my publishing company, TV and radio interviews, books, Google image search, and my Google+ information.

Have you Googled yourself lately? Sounds funny, but it's something you need to do at least on a monthly basis. You need to know what's out there in the world attached to your name. If someone writes a bad review, it's very difficult to remove that from internet search engines. So make sure you have a positive online presence first. If you see something negative, combat it with multiple blog entries, press releases, and other means to push that down from the first page of Google.

Fun fact: there are 75 other Tara Richters out there in the world. However, I dominate Google because I put in the ground work. I know how to get those other chicks pushed down and get my name up.

About Tara | Richter Publishing

https://richterpublishing.com/about/ ▾

Tara Richter is the President of **Richter** Publishing LLC. She specializes in helping business owners how to write their non-fiction story in 4 weeks & publish a book in order to become an expert in their industry. She has been featured on CNN, ABC, Daytime TV, FOX, SSN, Channel 10 ...

Tara Richter will be giving Keynote Speech at Keiser University's ...

https://richterpublishing.com/.../tara-richter-will-be-giving-keynote-speech-at-keiser-u... ▾

Jun 9, 2017 - This evening, **Tara Richter**, will be the keynote speaker at Keiser University's graduation ceremony! She will be telling her journey as an ...

Tara Richter | Keep St. Pete Lit

keepstpetelit.org/tara-richter/ ▾

Tara Richter: Richter_Tara richterpublishing.com. I'm an author of 6 books and also a publisher and have published to date 10 books of other authors in the ...

Amazon.com: Tara Richter: Books, Biography, Blog, Audiobooks, Kindle

https://www.amazon.com/Tara-Richter/e/B00CGKD8FG ▾

Visit Amazon.com's **Tara Richter** Page and shop for all **Tara Richter** books. Check out ... Write a Book in 4 Weeks (Richter Publishing) (Volume 3) by **Tara Richter** ...

Tara Richter

www.tararichter.com/ ▾

Check out this GoDaddy hosted webpage! http://tararichter.com.

Images for Tara Richter

→ More images for Tara Richter

Report images

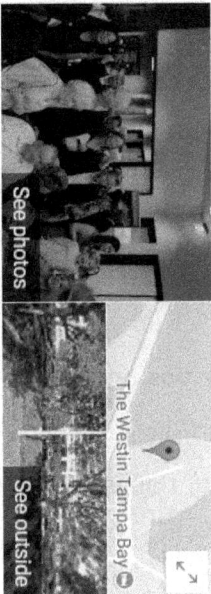

See photos   See outside

The Westin Tampa Bay ❶

Richter Publishing LLC ☆

5.0 ★★★★★ 7 Google reviews

Book publisher in Tampa, Florida

[Website]   [Directions]

Address: 3001 N Rocky Point Dr E Suite 200, Tampa, FL 33607

Hours: Closed now ▾

Phone: (727) 940-7647

Suggest an edit

Know this place? Answer quick questions

Reviews from the web

5/5   Facebook   5 votes

📱 **Send to your phone**   [Send]

Reviews

5/5   [Edit your review]   [Add a photo]

Feedback

ONLINE IMPACT

Once you have a book, opportunities arise. You can write articles for online sites, magazines, and newspapers. The more articles you have published, the more it will increase your profile, the more it will solidify your expertise.

The internet is a powerful networking and marketing tool. Anything posted on the internet with your name on it will be linked to you through Google Search Engine Spiders. So having a great online profile is beneficial. Once your book is published, you will be listed on various outlets. You may be surprised at who contacts you in regards to your expertise. TV producers still reach out to me for books that I have written and published years ago. I had producers from London contact me to do an episode on BBC America with my Dating Jungle Series. They were filming a show in Florida and were looking for an Dating Expert. Their Google searches kept coming back to me because I am really good with SEO (Search Engine Optimization). I also had three books published one the topic. However, I do not do anything with that series anymore because I'm running my publishing house fulltime. But you do not turn down an opportunity to be on BBC America! So I took them up on their offer. These are the doors that books open for you.

Set up your future connections with a strong online presence. For more tips on how to solidify your online presence, get a copy of my guide "Blog Your Book into Existence." It dives more into the technical side of things like SEO, blogging, key terms, and understanding Google Search Engine Algorithms.

LEVERAGING YOUR BOOK FOR TV / RADIO

Unless you're famous, TV shows, radio shows, and podcasts need a reason to interview you. For the average person, the book gives them a reason to be newsworthy.

I wanted to write for magazines about my experience in the dating world. However, I had no credibility. When I published my book, the magazines came to me—USA Today, Beverley Hills Times, Lady Luck, Digital Romance. My book was blasted on Daytime TV, ABC, CNN, Channel 10 News, and Fox 6 News. Without the book, I was a nobody. With the book, I had leverage.

If you have a business, you want PR attention. Books are your ticket. You can now talk about your company in the public stratosphere.

In 2014, politician Charlie Crist used his book tour to gain national attention. He was interviewed on Bill O'Reilly and Stephen Colbert. He appeared on multiple TV programs in the state of Florida. The Tampa Bay Times estimated his total free publicity was worth a whopping $693,351.53!

Hire a PR professional. Once you have a book out, you want an aggressive marketing campaign. You'll want to blast out emails to the proper media contacts, so they can get in contact with you. It's not as easy as it sounds. But it's not impossible. Media personalities love interviewing authors. The sudden publicity is a source for a surge of customers.

Surviving the Dating Jungle
Avoid the knight in shining armor.

CNN Senior Editor John DeDakis of "The Situation Room with Wolf Blizter"

&

Author Tara Richter joint book signing at the Ritz Carlton

FINDING LOVE ONLINE: SMARTPHONE SWEETIES

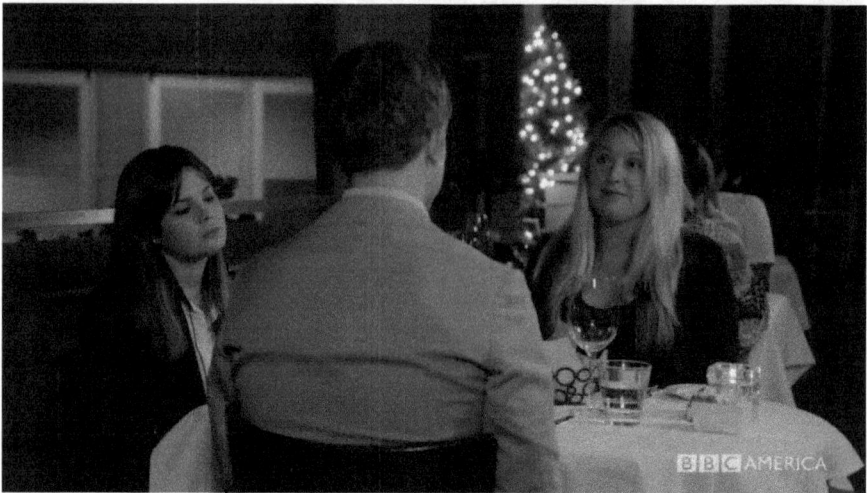

Review:

Tip #1: Publish a book to become an expert. Publish multiple books to become a mainstay.

Tip #2: Maintain a positive presence online.

Tip #3: Use your book as an advertising tool for your company.

FINAL THOUGHTS

I know writing a book isn't easy. Having it published is another feat. Then marketing is a pain in the ass. I know because I have been doing it the last seven years professionally, but I've been writing books my entire life. Most of them stayed in my computer or sat on my desk as ideas and half-finished pieces of work. Honestly, if someone told me 20 years ago when I was in college doing short stories for my creative writing class I would someday open my own publishing house, I would have called them crazy. But if I look back to my childhood, I used to create little books with rubber paste and ribbons since I was probably five years old. It was in my blood to do this. I just had to figure it out get more high tech than crayons.

You know when you are meant to do something. You can feel it in your veins. If you are reading this book then you have that inner voice that keeps telling you to share your stories with the world. I'm here to help make that come true. I love what I do and I know it's my purpose here on earth, to share other's stories with the world.

I hope this guide helps you along the way. You can make your dream a reality. You can become a published author.

Sincerely,

Tara Richter

ABOUT THE AUTHOR

Tara Richter is the President of Richter Publishing LLC and specializes in helping business owners write and publish their nonfiction story in 4 weeks in order to become an expert in their industry. She has been featured on CNN, ABC, Daytime TV, FOX, SSN, Channel 10 News, USA TODAY, BBC and many other media outlets.

Her degree is in Graphic Design and she worked in the copy and print industry in the Silicon Valley. She has written and published 15 of her own books in just a few short years. Tara now has published many other authors all over the world including Anthony Amos & celebrity entrepreneur, Kevin Harrington, Shark from ABC's "Shark Tank" with their joint book, "How to Catch a Shark." She has also worked with many doctors, lawyers, non-profits and Fortune 500 Corporations such as Blooming Inc.

Richter Publishing has streamlined the complex writing and publishing industry so anyone can become a published author quickly.

AWARDS:

2013 Finalist for Tampa Bay's Business Woman of the Year Award

2014 Nominee for Tampa's Up & Coming Businesses

2015 Nominee for 2015 Iconic Woman of the Year

2015 Finalist for Best in Biz

2015 Amazon Best Selling Author & #1 Amazon Hot New Release

2016 Recipient of H.E.R.O. Award

2017 Commencement Speaker for Keiser University Graduation

2019 Nominee for Tampa Bay's Corporate Philanthropy Award

2020 Amazon Best Seller for the title, "How to Run a Business During a Zombie Apocalypse"

2021 Florida Authors and Publishers Association (FAPA) Book Award Winner Business Category for "How to Run a Business During a Zombie Apocalypse"

To see Tara's other books, scan this code:

SCAN ME

OUR SERVICES

At Richter Publishing LLC we have a variety of services to help you during your writing and publishing journey. Use this guide to do everything yourself, but if you get stuck along the way, we are here to assist you. We offer everything from ghost writing to publishing and Amazon Best Seller marketing campaigns. https://richterpublishing.com/contact-us/

Or contact us at:

Email: richterpublishing@icloud.com

Phone: 727-301-8204